Stoic Ethics: Our Duty To Each Other

Stoic Ethics: Our Duty To Each Other

Julie Favre

Translated by
Will Johncock

Planktos Press

Published by Planktos Press.
Sydney, Australia.
www.planktospress.com

Copyright © 2024

All rights reserved. Except for brief quotations in critical publications or reviews, no part of this book may be reproduced in any manner without prior permission from the publisher.

Paperback ISBN: 978-1-922931-08-5
eBook ISBN: 978-1-922931-09-2

Stoic Ethics: Our Duty To Each Other was originally published in French as the *Preface*, and the chapter *Devoirs de l'homme envers ses semblables*, in the book *La morale des Stoïciens (1888)*, by Félix Alcan Publishing, Paris.

Contents

	Preface	i
1.	Human Fraternity	1
2.	Justice	11
3.	Passive Charity	29
4.	Active Charity	63
	I. How To Give	79
	II. How To Receive	101

Preface

We do not claim to explain the doctrine of the Stoics. Eminent masters have made it known to us with a talent worthy of such a noble cause, even if their learned studies have not made more accessible the prodigious height to which these great types of humanity rose through their virtue. Those who admire the Stoics most always see them soaring in sublime regions, where it seems impossible to follow them. They even say, that the more they respect the Stoics, the more they despair of imitating them. Mixed with the sincere and profound veneration that they feel for such a lofty virtue is a kind of fear of something that is above, if not beyond, human nature. Such is the general impression that we have made of the Stoics. Is the cause to be found in a false idea of the force of fortitude, the greatness of which is not diminished even by errors and excesses? Or is it in human weakness, which tries to excuse its inaction by acknowledging that it is powerless to achieve the good? We are led to believe that it is as much incomplete knowledge as it is weak will that prevents most admirers of the Stoics from becoming their imitators. They conclude from certain acts or words, separated from what precedes and follows them, that these heroes were giants in the moral domain, that they had received from heaven an extraordinary virtue to accomplish their gigantic work, and that this virtue, which had its raison d'être in centuries of tyranny and corruption, would be excessive and even monstrous today. While paying tribute to the indomitable energy and inflexible firmness of these noble witnesses to human dignity, they reproach them for having risen to such great heights only by ignoring or suppressing the most legitimate sentiments.

We have the firm conviction that a thorough study of the writings of the

Stoics would correct such an erroneous opinion. So, in the hope of awakening the desire to enter into communication with the thought of these great masters of humanity, we have tried to collect what seems to us to best characterise their morality. Our modest efforts would be only too well rewarded if these texts could convey to the reader's soul what they have conveyed to ours, namely, that the Stoics did not outgrow humanity, that they understood and respected human nature, and that they loved it above all else, since they wanted it to be great and worthy of its divine nature. They saw its greatness in its free will, which they strove to preserve in themselves and in others. They worked to free themselves from everything that did not depend on free will, to perfect their souls in the image of God, to contribute to universal harmony through justice, benevolence, and love. If, in their holy passion for good, they sometimes show themselves to be too ardent, impatient, and absolute, who would reproach them? If, in struggling against evil, they often seem insensitive to pain, it is because they are exalted by the greatness of the end that they are pursuing. If they take detachment to extremes, if they are strong to the point of appearing inhuman, who can deny them admiration, even in their exaggerations? If their sense of dignity makes them proud and even haughty in the face of all servitude, who would not respect them for it more?

We might be reproached for sometimes drawing parallels between the texts of the Stoics and those of the Christian books. But the Gospel loses none of its authority with this comparison. The analogy we have seen, between certain precepts of Stoic morality and the teachings of Christian morality, clearly shows us the unity of morality and the intimate relationships between divine law and human conscience. We do not believe that it is a lack of respect for Christianity to recognise that, across all the ages, God has made for humanity some revelation of moral truth. He rewards upright hearts that sincerely seek the truth in order to be guided by it, in giving them a superior understanding of all things that have to do with the soul, its origin, and its destiny. This is how Socrates, Plato, and the Stoics, rose, by the rectitude of their consciences and the integrity of their lives, to more perfect moral notions than most of those who were instructed by the law of Moses. Because these faithful servants of God are neither of the Old nor of the New Testament, must we doubt that they spoke and acted by divine inspiration? Was not the law of God written on their consciences and in their hearts? Does not Saint Paul himself bear witness to them when he says that the uncircumcised who fulfil the law draw their praise from God? We would much rather be excluded one hundred times from the community of the faithful with these Christian hearts, than be admitted there with the narrow-minded people who exclude them. The moral idea of the Stoics does not seem to us to noticeably differ from that of the Christians. The work of the Christians is to "strip the old human of their passions and lusts and to clothe the new human created in true justice and holiness." The work of the Stoics is to free the soul from all the desires of lower nature and to transform it into the likeness of God. Even if the terms are different, the idea is identical. It is true after all, that for the Stoics life is an ascent, while for the Christians it is a rising.

The idea of moral decay is not found in the Stoic doctrine, which speaks only of the perpetual conflict between our two natures. But even if they do not pronounce the word "grace" from God, these valiant athletes of humanity do not expect everything from their own strength. "The beginning of philosophy, at least for those who are properly attached to it," says Epictetus, "is the feeling of our infirmity and weakness in indispensable things." And elsewhere, he says; "Remember God and call upon him in a storm!" The Stoics are criticised for having thought more about making the human a God than about making the human like God. Nothing, in their teachings, has given us this impression. The generous exaltation that produces in them "the passion for honesty," as well as the humility inspired by the sense of their own imperfections, constantly elevates their souls toward the author of all things. Not to mention that we believe their words exceeded their thoughts when they say that the human, through constancy in virtue, would surpass God. There is perhaps a great deal of pride in their conviction of the omnipotence of the human will, but they never separate the human from God, who makes humanity great and to whom they attribute all their virtue. If we had to choose between confidence, however exaggerated, in the will, and the inertia of a timid soul that waits for a movement of grace even to have the strength to will, we would not hesitate for a moment to side with the Stoics. However, we believe that the truth lies between these two extremes, and this is the attitude of the true Christian, who understands that it is necessary to begin by acting with the little strength they have, so that God multiplies it for them by his grace.

We are so convinced of the power of Stoicism that we wish the soul had been initiated into the freedom of Christianity by the strong morality of Stoicism. Mercy, grace, and love of God, can only be understood after having felt all the rigours of the inflexible, perfect law. We do not fully understand weakness until we have tried to satisfy all the demands of our conscience. A person's will must have been at grips with its selfish desires and passions in order that they can persuade themselves that, in this struggle with themselves, they need a more powerful helper if they are to triumph, and that unless they find that helper outside themselves, above themselves, they cannot claim victory. It doesn't seem to be a good idea to us to insist on forfeiture at the moment when the soul is born into moral life. The young child cannot understand it until they have had some experience of the struggle. By always repeating to them that humans are weak and incapable of doing good, we risk accustoming the child to a vain phraseology, or of stifling in them the desire to use their strength. All the power and dignity of a human lies in their free will. It is therefore important that they exercise this will, and, in order to make them act, they must be persuaded that to will is to be able. What is to be dreaded most in education is not confidence in the strength of the will, but rather the inertia of a weak or timid soul. The noble pride that comes from a sense of strength promptly moderates itself in its excess, as a person learns from experience that they are not invincible by their own strength. But it is difficult to remedy a paralysed will that allows the instincts of an inferior nature to grow without resistance, and is content to moan about its infirmity, while always waiting for the miracle that might eventually release it.

People complain about the general absence of characters. They search for original minds and vigorous souls. Yet when, from the heart of the crowd of average natures that a uniform education has shaped, a powerful nature emerges that has the courage to be itself, thanks to the inflexible principles it has given itself, some people call it ancient, others chimerical, and even often suspect it of being struck by dementia or at least possessed of the mania for singularity. It would take a flood of Stoicism to submerge the artificial life that humans have made for themselves, and speak a life more in keeping with their true nature. These humans were true, those who had such a firm conviction of the excellence of their souls that they valued as nothing anything that did not contribute to its perfection. They were consistent with their spiritualist principles, they subordinated material life to these principles and reduced their needs to the strictly necessary. They knew how to endure work, not in order to obtain greater pleasures for themselves, but to discipline their souls. They resigned themselves to suffering, and endured the struggle to purify their divine nature. They were not greedy for honours or external distinctions, but they aspired to the true greatness that comes from virtue. They did not follow the multitude or court their votes, but thirsted for the approval of their conscience. They did not isolate themselves in brutal egotism or fierce and haughty virtue, but strove to be living and active members of the great human family. We see only the true Christian as being superior to the Stoic, such as depicted by Pascal when he stated: "No one is as happy, reasonable, virtuous, nor lovable, as a true Christan." Are these Christians, who "shine like torches in the world, carrying the word of life," any less rare than the gentle yet proud Stoics, who remind us by precept and example that we must live as humans?

May a spiritualist, charitable religion, and a liberal education, respectful of human dignity, increase the number of true Stoics and true Christians. The one and the other are made to meet and get along in a common veneration of the human soul and moral law, in an equal submission to God, and in the charity for humankind.

Julie Favre
Widow of Jules Favre, born Velten.
Sèvres
19 avril 1887.

Chapter 1

Human Fraternity

According to the Stoics, humans were made to live in society. It is to society that we owe our strength and security. Everyone is a member of this great body, whose salvation depends on the love and mutual support of all its parts. Seneca views the duties of a human toward their fellow humans first from the point of view of their very usefulness. Humans, weak and naked, receive everything from society. "From where comes our safety," Seneca says, "if not from the reciprocity of services? The only guarantee of our life, its only defence against sudden attacks, is this trade in benefits. Just as all members must accord with each other, because all are interested in the conversation of each, so all members must save each other, because they are born to live together."

However, Seneca also raises higher considerations: "Nature has made all of us parents by creating us from the same material and for the same purpose. Nature inspired us with a mutual love and made us all sociable. It is Nature that established justice and equity. According to its constitutions, it is a greater evil to give an insult than to receive one, and it is by Nature's order that our hands must always be ready to give help. Let us have this verse in our mouths and in our hearts:

I am a human and hold nothing human outside myself."

The duties of justice therefore follow from the common origin of all humans, from their fraternity. Epictetus also insists on this kinship that Marcus Aurelius calls "a holy kinship that unites every human with all of humankind, a kinship not of blood or birth, but of participation in the same intelligence." Social virtues for them consist not in acts of fairness and kindness, but in the love that inspires the acts. The principle therefore is no longer the interest in it, the need to support one another through an exchange of good services, but given that humans are all children of God, they must love each other and not grow weary of doing good. Saint Paul uses no other language. Seneca thinks it is unnecessary to list what humans must do and what they must avoid. He believes he says it all in reminding us that we are all "members of the same body." These words, in effect, contain all the precepts that humans should observe among themselves. To define them would be to limit them, and yet justice and love have no limits, so he states; "The hands must always be ready." For the hands to open and not grow weary, the heart must be open. It is not in the name of God's love for humans that the Stoics order us to love one another, but in the name of "the union, the harmony, of all nature." To separate oneself from the whole through injustice, hatred, and aversion, "is to throw oneself outside of the union that consists of our nature." It is, in other words, to separate oneself from God himself, who is harmony, that is to say, love.

"Nothing dissolves and destructs the agreement of the human race, like ingratitude. From where does your safety come, if not from the reciprocity of services? The only guarantee of our life, its only defence against sudden attacks, is this trade in benefits. Suppose that we were isolated, what would we be? The prey of animals, the weakest victim, the easiest blood to spill. Other animals have enough strength to defend themselves. Those born to wander, to lead a solitary life, are armed. Humans are surrounded only by their weakness. Neither sharp fingernails nor powerful teeth make it something to dread. Naked and disabled, it is society that protects the human. God has given humans two powers that have made a precarious being the strongest, reason and society, and the human who, taken separately, would be inferior to all, is here the master of the world. It is society that has given humans ownership of all the animals. Born on land, it is society that has extended the human empire over a foreign climate, and wanted humans to dominate even the sea. It is society that repels the assaults of disease, prepares supports for old age, and provides consolation against distress. It is society that makes us courageous and enables us to invoke its patronage against fortune. Destroy society, and you break the unity of the human race, on which life depends. You will destroy it if you maintain that ingratitude must not be avoided for its own sake, but for fear of something external." (Seneca, *On Benefits*, 4, xviii).

"Just as all members must accord with each other, because all are interested in the conversation of each, so all members must save each other, because they are born to live together. The only salvation for society is the mutual love and support of each of its members." (Seneca, *On Anger*, 2, xxxi).

"It is a small thing to not harm someone that we should help. What praise it is for a human to be kind toward another. Should we teach humans to lend a hand to someone who is shipwrecked, to show the way to someone who is lost, and to share one's bread with someone who is starving? Why should I amuse myself by deducing everything that must be done or avoided, since in a few words I can teach everyone the duties of humans in this form. This world, you see, which encloses things divine and things human, is but one. We are members of this great body. Nature made us all parents by creating us from one and the same material and for one and the same purpose. It inspired us with mutual love and made us all helpful. It is Nature that established justice and equity.

According to its constitutions it is a greater evil to make an insult than to receive one. It is by Nature's order that mothers must always be ready to give help. Let us have this verse in our mouths and in our hearts:

I am a human and hold nothing human outside myself. We are born to live together, in common, our society is a vault of stones bound together which would fall if the one did not support the other." (Seneca, *Letters*, xcv).

"If you have ever seen a hand, a foot, or a head, cut off, separated from the rest of the body, this is the image of what is done by someone, as much as it is within the one who does not accept events, who removes themselves from the great whole, or who does some harmful action to society. You have thrown yourself out of this union which made up your nature. Your nature had made you a part of the whole, you have now cut yourself off from it. But here there is something admirable, you are allowed to re-enter this union, which God did not grant to other parts, namely: to return to their place after having been separated and cut off. Consider what goodness is necessary in order to grant humans this prerogative. God has afforded the human either never to be torn from his whole, or, when the human has been torn from it, to allow them to rejoin it, to adhere to it, to take back their place in it." (Marcus Aurelius, viii, 34).

"A branch detached from the branch to which it was held is necessarily detached from the whole tree. Thus, a human separated from a human is cut off from the best of society. It is a stranger who cuts off the branch, but it is the human itself who separates itself from their neighbour through hatred and aversion, unaware that at the same time they have cut themselves off from the whole city." (Marcus Aurelius, xi, 8).

"You have forgotten what holy kinship unites each human with all humankind, a kinship not of blood or birth, but of participation in the same intelligence." (Marcus Aurelius, xii, 26).

Chapter 2

Justice

Justice, for the Stoics, is not that negative virtue which consists in not doing harm to others. They give it the broadest meaning, for them it is almost perfection, the outward manifestation of the virtue with which the soul is instilled, and as they conceived it, it seems to me to be inseparable from love. It was not the Stoics who devised the subtle distinction between strict and broad duties. The Stoics were not minds of categories and classes, everything for them was absolute. For the Stoics, one is either just or not just. One is just not by conforming to social law in all outward acts, but by making one's will just. For this to be so, the habit of the soul must be perfect. Seneca calls justice "an excellent and divine thing which only looks to the usefulness of others, and desires nothing other than to serve everyone… Above all, let each person persuade and say to themselves: It is necessary that I am just without expecting any reward. I even want people to say: I am obliged to cultivate this beautiful virtue without any consideration for my particular interests. Because, in doing a just action, one must not claim to be something other than just." It is therefore always the intention, the feeling that serves as the motive, that Seneca goes back to when assessing actions. True justice excludes all thought of self-interest, as well as of ambition and vanity. Seneca says that it acts "to please itself." I believe this means that the just human has no other concern than to satisfy the feeling of justness which is in them, and which is infinite. It seems to me that Seneca goes as far as possible in his conception of justice, since he even understands the joy of being persecuted for the sake of justice or being just: "I assure you," he says, "that often it is necessary to be just at the expense of one's reputation. Then, if you know how to take it well, the bad noise that will result from a good deed will give you a holy pleasure." The idea of justice is therefore so far above all external considerations that it often seems to contradict them all. In practice a human must be inflexible in order to act according to how they are persuaded by their conscience, despite the opposition of other humans. Marcus Aurelius considers as just only "the action which has as its goal the good of society." For him, justice is the source of other virtues, "because," he says, "we would not know how to observe justice if we became passionate about indifferent things, or if we gave in to error, prejudices, and inconsistency." The one who sins, wrongs their own soul, and Marcus Aurelius finds them more worthy of pity than the victim of their injustice.

Like Seneca, Marcus Aurelius shows that it is not only in action that one can be unjust, but also in feeling, thought, and judgement.

To distrust others, to suspect them without cause, to misinterpret certain more or less indifferent acts, is to be unjust. So many of these injustices of thought have their source in selfishness, egoism, and pride! The self, the ego, so demanding and susceptible, sees faults with everything that seems to harm its exorbitant claims: "Let us look at things more simply," Seneca tells us, "and judge them with benevolence… Let us believe only what meets the eye, what is obvious to us, and, every time we recognise that our suspicions are ill-founded, let us reprimand our gullibility." But the fair-mindedness of the Stoics shows above all in the leniency of their judgements of others. Seneca, recognising the unfairness of using a single weight and measure in regard to so many different minds and dispositions, urges us to examine the character and intention of those that we see acting around us. He takes into account differences of age, culture, sex, condition, etc., and proves that most of our unjust judgements are caused by the encroachments of the ego. "It is the effect of too great a self-esteem. We persuade ourselves that, even for our enemies, we must be inviolable. Each human has in their heart the pretentions of a king, and wants to give themselves all power over others, without granting others any power over themselves." He severely condemns those who malevolently scrutinise the conduct of other humans, who turn their thoughts away from themselves and show themselves to be hard and merciless in regard to the smallest faults, and often even concerning indifferent things: "In others," he tells them, "you notice a little redness, and you yourself are covered in ulcers." Doesn't this phrase express very forcefully the same idea as the pot calling the kettle black? We find it in Epictetus with just as much force: "Before you know the motive for their decision," he says, "how do you know they are doing wrongly?… Do not praise or criticise anyone for what we have in common with everyone else. Do it only for their opinions and their intentions, because those alone are what belong to ourselves, and those alone make our actions honourable or shameful… If you eradicate or reduce in yourself malignancy, the inclination to gossip, to act in haste… what a great opportunity for sacrifice there is!" Marcus Aurelius, to be fair in his judgements, tries to put himself in the place of those who he judges, to examine their principles and opinions. As a result, he comes to understand their way of acting. But he is especially dedicated to discovering their good qualities: "the activity of this one, the modesty of that one, the liberality of that other one, and so on, for there is nothing," he says, "that gives pleasure like the image of the virtues that shine in the behaviours of those who live with us and that stick out before our eyes. So always have their virtues present."

"The law is the queen of all things divine

and human. It must be the arbiter of good and evil, the rule of just and unjust, the sovereign and master by nature of sentient animals, command what must be done, and forbid the contrary." (Chrysippus).

"Virtue requires knowledge of itself, and of everything else. This must be learned first, in order to then learn what will we should have. Action will not be right if the will is not also, since it is the will that produces the action, and this will cannot be right if the habit of the soul, from which the will is produced, is not right. Finally, the habit of the soul will not be perfect if it does not know well all the rules of life, if it does not soundly judge all things, and if it does not reduce them to their right value. In order to always want the same thing, it is necessary to want what is true." (Seneca, *Letters*, xcv).

"Let them teach me what an excellent and divine thing justice is, which only looks to the usefulness of others, and desires nothing other than to serve everyone. Justice does nothing out of ambition, nor vanity, but only in order to please itself. Above all, let each person convince themselves, and say to themselves: I must be just without expecting any reward. I also want people to say: I am obligated to cultivate this beautiful virtue without any consideration for my particular interests. For in doing a just act, we must not claim anything other than to be just. Remember what I told you a little earlier. There is no point in lots of people knowing that you are just. Someone who publicises their virtue is not working for virtue, but for glory. You only want to be just in order to receive honour, however I assure you that often you must be just at the expense of your reputation. Then, if you know how to take it well, the bad noise that will result from a good action will give you secret pleasure." (Seneca, *Letters*, cxiii).

"The person who sins, sins against themselves. The injustice committed falls on the perpetrator, since they make themselves unjust." (Marcus Aurelius, ix, 4).

"Often one commits injustice without doing anything, it is not action alone that is unjust." (Marcus Aurelius, ix, 5).

"Peace of mind regarding the things that come from an external cause, justice in the actions of which you, yourself, are the cause. I mean that every desire, every action, must have no other goal than the good of society, because that is what is in accordance with your nature." (Marcus Aurelius, ix, 31).

"Justice is the source of the other virtues, because we would not know how to observe justice if we became passionate about indifferent things, or if we gave in to error, prejudices, and inconsistency." (Marcus Aurelius, xi, 10).

"We must banish from the soul all

suspicion, all conjecture, the source of unjust anger. One such soul greeted me impolitely, another embraced me coldly, this other one abruptly interrupted a sentence I had started, that other one did not invite me to a meal, and the face of this other person seemed ungracious. There will never be a lack of excuses for suspicions. Let us look more simply at things and judge them with kindness. Let us believe only what meets the eye, what is obvious, and every time we recognise that our suspicions are ill-founded, let us reprimand our gullibility. This serenity will give us the habit of not believing easily." (Seneca, *On Anger*, 2, xxiv).

"There are certain things of which we are a witness. In this case, let's examine the character and intention of those who do those things. Is it a child? We forgive their age, they do not know if they are doing wrong. Is it a father? Perhaps he has done enough good for us to have earned the right to an offence, or maybe it is just another act of service that we take for an insult. Is it by order? Who could, without injustice, be irritated by what is necessary? Is it in retaliation? It is not to be offended, to suffer what you first caused to suffer. Is it a judge? Respect their decision more than your own. Is it a king? If he strikes you, and you are guilty, give in to justice. If you are innocent, give in to fortune. Is it an animal without reason, or a similar being? You assimilate yourself to it by becoming irritated. Is it an illness, a disaster? It will pass more quickly if you withstand it. Is it a god? You are wasting your time and efforts getting angry with him, as much as if you invoked his anger against another person. Did a good person insult you? Don't believe it. Is it a nasty person? Don't be surprised, someone else will punish them for what they have done to you, and already they have punished themselves through the mistake that they made.

Two circumstances arouse anger. Firstly, when it seems to us that we have been insulted, and secondly, when it seems to us that we have been treated unjustly. Humans consider to be unjust, certain things that they do not deserve to suffer, or other things that they did not expect. We judge to be unjust what is unforeseen. What outrages us the most is what happens against expectation and hope. It is for no other reason that the smallest things offend us in our hearts, and that, in a friend, we call negligence an insult.

'Why,' it is asked, 'are we so sensitive to the insults of an enemy?' It is that they come against our expectations, or that they exceed them. It is the effect of too great a self-esteem. We persuade ourselves that, even for our enemies, we must be inviolable. Each human has in their heart the pretentions of a king, and wants to give themselves all power over others, without granting others any power over themselves. It is therefore either ignorance of things or the presumption that makes us irritable. Ignorance, for is it surprising that the wicked do evil? What is strange about an enemy harming, a friend offending, a son forgetting, a slave neglecting? Fabius thought it was the most pitiful excuse for a general to say: 'I did not think of that.' I think it is just as pitiful for any human. Think of everything, plan for everything, even the best characters have their rough edges. Human nature produces insidious friends. It produces ungrateful ones, greedy ones, and impious ones. In your judgements on the morals of a sole person, think of public morals. When you are most pleased with yourself, you must be the most afraid. When everything seems calm, there is no shortage of storms, but they lie dormant." (Seneca, *On Anger*, 2, xxx).

"Do you have the spare time to dig through the miseries of others and pass judgement about someone? Why is this philosopher staying offshore? Why does this one dine so sumptuously? In others you notice a little redness, and you yourself are covered in ulcers. It is as if you were joking about the blemishes and the warts on the most beautiful bodies, as the one devoured by a hideous leprosy. Reproach Plato for having demanded money, Aristotle for having received it, Democritus for having made little use of it, Epicurus for having squandered it, and reproach myself incessantly for Alcibiades and Phaedra. Oh, you will be too happy in your apprenticeship when, for the first time, you will be given the chance to imitate our vices! Why don't you contemplate instead your own evils, which are stabbing you from all directions? Some besiege you from outside, others consume your insides. No, human affairs have not reached this point, even though you know, through your own situation, that you have much leisure left, and that you have time to wag your tongue to accuse better people than yourself." (Seneca, *On The Happy Life*, xxvii).

"Someone is bathing early. Don't say, 'it is wrong,' but say, 'it is early.' Someone drinks a lot of wine. Don't say, 'it is wrong,' but say, 'it is a lot.' For before you know the reason for their decision, from where do you know whether they are doing wrong? So it will not happen that you see and understand one thing, and give a verdict on another." (Epictetus, *Manual*, xiv).

"Do not praise or criticise anyone for what we have in common with everyone else. Do it only for their opinions and their intentions, because those alone are what belong to ourselves, and those alone make our actions honourable or shameful. If you eradicate or reduce in yourself malignancy, the inclination to gossip, to act in haste, the habit of obscene talk, thoughtlessness, nonchalance, if you are no longer troubled by what troubled you before, or if you are less troubled by it, then you will be able to celebrate a feast each day, today for having acted well in this case, tomorrow in another. What a great opportunity for sacrifice there is, far more wonderful than from combat or the office of a praetor! For these are things that come to you from yourself alone and from the Gods, whereas you must remember who gave you those latter things, to whom they are given, and for what purpose.

If you are nourished by these reflections, what will it matter to you in what place you will be happy, in what place you will be pleasing to God! Is what we receive from the Gods not the same everywhere? Do they not have the same eyes everywhere on what is done?" (Epictetus, *Discourses*, iv, 4).

"When you want to give yourself pleasure, recall to your mind the qualities of those who live with you, the activity of this one, the modesty of that one, the liberality of that other one, and so on. For there is nothing that gives pleasure like the image of the virtues that shine in the behaviours of those who live with us and that stick out before our eyes. So always have their virtues present." (Marcus Aurelius, vi, 48).

"When you meet someone, say to yourself immediately: What are this person's principles about true good and evil. Because, if they have certain opinions about pleasure and pain, about what causes one or the other, about glory, disgrace, death, and life, there is nothing surprising or strange to me that they might do what they therefore do, and I will remember that it is necessary that they do so." (Marcus Aurelius, viii, 14).

Chapter 3

Passive Charity

Leniency, Support, Patience, Gentleness

The Stoics practise leniency through justice as much as through charity. They hold that a person does not have the right to condemn those who sin, nor to avenge the offences they incur from other people, since they do the same things. The evil that we see done should bring our thoughts back to ourselves, and remind us of the errors that we have committed: "It is not for a wise person," says Seneca, "to hate those who lose their way, otherwise they would be hating themselves. Let this person remember how many of our actions need leniency… A fair judge does not pass a different sentence in their own cause than in that of a stranger. No, there is no one who can entirely absolve themselves, and every person who claims to be innocent invokes the testimony of others and not their own conscience… We are wicked, we live among wicked people. Only one thing can make us calm down: a treaty of mutual leniency." It is impossible to make it clearer than this: the right of every person is to support, and to be supported by, others. But the Stoics do not limit themselves to showing that justice and equity demand leniency and forgiveness. They also recommend these features to us in the name of the love that should unite all people. Without pronouncing the name of charity, "which excuses and endures all things," they make us feel that all their words are imbued with it. In their eyes, those who sin, are all the more worthy of pity. They regard them as ignorant people whom we must try to enlighten, misguided people whom we must bring back through gentleness and patience, sick people whom we must pity, love, support, and heal.

"Why," says Seneca, "do you put up with the emotional outbursts of a sick person, the words of a frenzied person, the blows of a child? Is it that they seem to you to not know what they are doing? What does it matter which illness causes them to talk and act unreasonably? Unreasonableness is an equal excuse for everyone." He also reproaches those who are irritated, and reminds them of the law of love: "Come on, you unfortunate creature, when are you going to love? Oh, what a good time you are wasting on bad things!" Not to forget the touching humility Epictetus feels, when people speak badly of him! "If you are told that someone has spoken badly about you, do not justify what they have said, just reply: They were without doubt unaware of my other faults, because if they were aware they would not have only spoken of those faults." You also should excuse those who do you wrong: "Remember," he says, "that they do it believing that they are doing the right thing." Show them that they are wrong, and you will see how they will stop doing wrong. Marcus Aurelus also, in the high position in which fortune had placed him, far from losing his sense of humanity, knew how to enter into the thoughts of everyone, and was not irritated by those who misunderstood his intentions. "If the sailors," he says, "insulted the captain, and the sick insulted their doctor, would it be for any other reason than to make them look for a way to save, for this one their passengers, for that one their sick." The Stoics are convinced that it is because people fail to understand the truth that they allow themselves to be led into evil. So they urge us to instruct those who are mistaken, to correct with kindness those who neglect their true interests. With what gentleness they speak of those who go astray! With what sincere charity also they remind us of our fraternal duties in regard to the weak, the ignorant, and the wicked! "Show therefore to this person," says Epictetus, "where the truth is, and you will see how they go." Speaking of the good person, he also says: "They will be patient with those who are not like themselves, they will be gentle with them, kind, lenient, as with ignorant people, who go astray in the most important matters. They will not be harsh with anyone, because they will be invested with the words of Plato: 'It is always in spite of itself that a soul is deprived of the truth.'" Marcus Aurelius goes further, he wants us to love even those who offend us.

But it is not only in the name of fraternal feelings that the Stoics ask for leniency for all humans, it is also in the name of God, who forgives so that we might forgive: "The gods, who are immortal," says Marcus Aurelius, "resign themselves without anger to putting up for countless centuries with such a great number of wicked people. Even better, they take all kinds of care with them. But you, you who are soon going to cease to live, tire yourself out, and you do that when you are one of these wicked people."

It is also in the name of self-respect that the Stoics urge us to not be irritated by those who do wrong, to pardon them and do good by them. "It is not nice," says Seneca, "to trade insult for insult... Revenge is a word which has nothing human about it... The person who returns the offence with only a little more apology sins more. This person loses their temper. You, contrarily, provoke it with your acts of generosity." Marcus Aurelius tells us that the best way to seek revenge is to not make yourself similar to the wicked: "Someone else behaves badly, what do I care? It's their business. Their ailments are their own, their actions are their own also. What I have now is what common nature wants me to have, and what I do is what my nature wants me to do." It was up to the gentlest of people to exalt the most invincible powers of kindness and gentleness, and to make us feel that these virtues, so worthy of our nature, far from being signs of weakness, are true strength, that which is possessed, which triumphs over all evil instincts and subjects the soul to the law of love. "It is not worthy of a human to lose their temper," he says, "gentleness and kindness, while they are more consistent with our nature, also have something more human about them. It is there we truly show strength and nerve, and not indignation and resentment." The most difficult victory, in fact, is the one we win over our ego and our pride. You must be strong to be gentle.

"'I cannot, you say, resign myself to it. It is too painful to suffer an insult.' You lie! For which person cannot bear an insult when they can bear anger? By doing so, you bear both anger and insult. Why do you put up with the emotional outbursts of a sick person, the words of a frenzied person, the blows of a child? Is it that they seem to you to not know what they are doing? What does it matter which illness it is that causes them to talk and act unreasonably?

Unreasonableness is an equal excuse for everyone. 'What! You say, the offence will go unpunished?' Suppose that you want it to be punished, however it will not be. The greatest punishment for evil is to have done it, and the most rigorous punishment is to be delivered to the torture of repentance.

We are all inconsiderate and lacking in foresight, we are all irresolute, quarrelsome, and ambitious. Why veil, in milder terms, the public plague? We are all wicked. So whatever we condemn in another, we each find in our own heart… Let us therefore be more tolerant of each other. We are wicked, we live among wicked people. Only one thing can make us calm down: a treaty of mutual leniency. This person has offended me, I have not offended them back, but perhaps you have already hurt someone, or you will hurt someone." (Seneca, *On Anger*, 3, xxxvi).

"Unless you light the fire of anger, and constantly renew the fuel that should fan its flames, it will go out itself and lose its violence every day. Is it not better that it is conquered by you than by itself? You lose your temper with this person, then with that person, with your slaves, then with those you have freed, with your parents, then with your children, with your acquaintances, and then with strangers. Everywhere, in fact, excuses abound if the heart does not intercede. Your fury will lead you from here to there, from there to even further, and as new stimuli arise at each step, your rage will be permanent. Come on, you unfortunate creature, when are you going to love? Oh, what a good time you are wasting on bad things! How sweet it would be, here and now, to make some friends, to appease your enemies, to serve the State, to give your care to your domestic affairs, rather than to go searching all over for what you can do to hurt someone's dignity, heritage, or person.

Let us distinguish between powerlessness and ill will. We will often forgive if we examine before we get angry. Far from that, we follow our first impulse, then despite the childishness of our outbursts, we persist with them, in order to not appear to inflame ourselves without cause. What is most unjust is that the injustice of anger makes it more stubborn. For we preserve it, we glorify it, as if the excess of anger was a proof of its justice. Oh, we would do much better to consider its initial motives in all their frivolity and insignificance. What we notice in the brute, we discover in the human: a ghost, a small thing, upsets them." (Seneca, *On Anger*, 3, xxviii).

"We must ponder the examples of anger in order to flee them. Contrarily, the examples of moderation and gentleness are those that we must follow. I am going to give you examples of people who lacked neither cause for anger, nor power to take revenge. Indeed, what could be easier for Antigone than to send to their torturous deaths two soldiers who, leaning against the royal tent, were doing what we willingly do, even though it is very dangerous: they were speaking badly of the king. Antigone's listener had heard everything, because the speakers were only separated from the listener by a simple cloth. He shook it gently, and said to them: 'Move further away, so that the king does not hear you.' The same listener, on a night march, having heard some soldiers cursing the king for having led them down a muddy and inextricable path, approached some of the most embarrassed and, after having helped free them without having made himself known, said: 'Curse Antigone for having led you into this tight spot, but also pray to the gods for the one who pulled you out of this quagmire.'

Is it a friend who offends us? They have done what they did not want to do. Is it an enemy? They have done what they should do. Let us give in to the wise, let us forgive the foolish. Finally, all of us should say that the wisest people fall into many faults, that no one is so circumspect that their modesty is not sometimes forgotten. No one is so composed whose seriousness is not led by the occasion to a few acts of vivacity, no one so cautious against insult that they do not fall into the fault that they want to avoid." (Seneca, *On Anger*, 3, xxxii).

"If you are told that someone has spoken badly about you, do not justify what they have said, just reply: 'They were without doubt unaware of my other faults, because if they were aware they would not have only spoken of those faults.'" (Epictetus, *Manual*, xxxiii).

"When someone does you wrong, or speaks badly about you, remember that they do it believing that they are doing the right thing. It is therefore not possible for them to follow your opinion, but instead only their own, and if their opinion is vicious, it is them who does badly, since it is them who is mistaken. Indeed, if someone believes a true syllogism to be false, it is not the syllogism that suffers, but

Passive Charity 41

the person who is mistaken. In starting from this point, you will behave with gentleness toward those who insult you, because you will say to yourself, with each insult: 'It seemed right to them.'" (Epictetus, *Manual*, xlii).

"Each thing has two handles: one makes it is easy to carry, the other makes it impossible. If your brother does you an injustice, do not take the thing from the side of the injustice, for that is the handle with which it cannot be carried. Rather, take it from this side: he is a brother, a man who has been fed with you, and you will take the thing from the side with which it can be carried." (Epictetus, *Manual*, xliii).

"Slave, can you not bear your brother, who has Jupiter for his first father, who is another son born of the same seed as you, and who has the same celestial origin? Because you have been placed in a higher position than others, are you going to rush to play the tyrant? Do you not remember who you are, and who you command? Do you not remember that it is to parents, to brothers by nature, to descendants of Jupiter? But I bought them, and they did not buy me! Do you see toward what you are looking? To the earth, to the abyss, to the wretched laws of the dead! You do not turn your look toward the laws of the gods." (Epictetus, *Discourses*, i, 13).

"Philosophers say that there is only one cause for people's assertions, the conviction that such and such a thing is true; one cause for their negations, the conviction that such and such a thing is false; one for their doubts, the conviction that such and such a thing is uncertain; one for their wants, the conviction that such and such a thing is right; one for their desires, the conviction that such and such a thing is useful to them. Where any of these are true, if it is impossible for them to desire anything other than what they deem appropriate, why should we lose our temper with most of them? They are swindlers and thieves, you say! What therefore are swindlers and thieves? People who are mistaken concerning what is good and what is bad. So, is it indignation or pity that they should inspire in you? Show them that they are wrong, and you will see how they stop doing evil. If they do not see their error, they have nothing they prefer to their opinion.

The wrongs of others must not produce an unnatural effect in you. Instead, have pity on them. Leave aside these words of anger and hatred, these exclamations of the masses: 'What a monster! What a scoundrel! What a horrible being!' Have you, for your part, ever become wise in one day? How severe on others are you!" (Epictetus, *Discourses*, i, 18).

"If it is clearly understood that a person's actions are only measured by what they seem to see (whether rightly or wrongly: if rightly, they are beyond reproach, if wrongly, they are the first to suffer from it, for it cannot be that error is on one side and suffering is on the other), there will be no anger nor indignation against anyone, no insults to anyone, no reproaches, no hatred, no hostility." (Epictetus, *Discourses*, i, 28).

"I know that the person I miss is in reality my relative, not because we are born of the same blood, of the same germ, but through our common participation in the spirit, through our common sampling of the divine nature. None of these people, therefore, can harm me, for none of them can throw me into what is shameful. Neither can I be angry with my relative, nor feel hatred for them, for we are born to lend ourselves to mutual work, like feet, like hands, like the upper and lower jaws. Consequently, hostility between people is against nature. To feel indignation or aversion in oneself is brutality." (Marcus Aurelius, ii).

"Do not use up the part which remains of

your life, in thoughts in which others are the object, unless you relate them to some purpose of public interest. Yes, you are failing to fulfill another duty. I say that to occupy your mind with what such and such a person is doing and why, and what they are saying, and what is in their soul, and what they are up to, etc., is to divert yourself from the study of the moderating principle that is in you. You must therefore exclude from the series of your thoughts, all chance, all frivolity and especially all curiosity and malice. You must accustom yourself to only have thoughts of such a nature that if someone suddenly asks you about what you are thinking, you can answer frankly: This or that. This is so that anyone can see, from your thoughts, that everything in you is simple and benevolent, that everything is from a sociable being, full of contempt for any thought which only has the object of pleasure, any pleasure whatsoever, as well as for any hatred, any envy, any suspicion, in short for any feeling whose opinion would make you blush with shame." (Marcus Aurelius, iii, 4).

"How hard it is not to allow people to gravitate toward those things which seem to them to be suitable and useful! And yet you do not grant them to do so, if I may say, when you are indignant that they commit faults. They do it only because they find those things suitable and useful to them! But they are mistaken. Thus, instruct them. Show them the fault, but without indignation." (Marcus Aurelius, vi, 27).

"Come to terms with the events that fate has destined for you, and as for the people with whom you share your life, love them, love them truly." (Marcus Aurelius, vi, 39).

"Accustom yourself to listen to the words of others without distraction, and enter, as far as possible, into the mind of the speaker." (Marcus Aurelius, vi, 53).

"If the sailors insulted the captain, and the

sick insulted their doctor, would it be for any other reason than to make them look for a way to save, for this one their passengers, for that one their sick." (Marcus Aurelius, vi, 55).

"Honey seems bitter to people with jaundice, those who have been bitten by a rabid dog fear water, little children think that their ball is a beautiful thing: why then should I be angry? Do you believe that a false opinion has less power than bile has over someone with jaundice, or venom over someone bitten by a rabid dog?" (Marcus Aurelius, vi).

"If someone gives you reason to think that they have done something wrong, say to yourself: Am I sure that it is a mistake? Or if the mistake is certain: Haven't they already admitted their guilt? The punishment is as sensitive for them as if they tore off their own face. To wish that the wicked not do badly, is to wish that there not be juice in the fig, that children not wail, that horses not neigh, and so on with other things that are necessary. What else could someone of such a character do? If you are skilful, then heal their character." (Marcus Aurelius, xii, 16).

"If someone sins against you, reflect immediately on what they must have thought of good or bad in order to do so. With this thought, you will have pity for them, you will no longer feel astonishment or anger. Either you have the same opinion as them about what is good and what is evil, or you will have another opinion, but analogous to theirs. You must therefore forgive. But, if you do not share their opinion about good and evil, it will be even easier for you to show leniency to someone who has a poor view." (Marcus Aurelius, vii, 26).

"The gods, who are immortal, resign themselves without anger to putting up for countless centuries with such a great number of wicked people. Even better, they take all kinds of care with them. But you, you who are soon going to cease to live, tire yourself out, and you do that when you are one of these wicked people." (Marcus Aurelius, vii, 70).

"If it's up to you, why are you doing it? If it's someone else's doing, who are you going to accuse? The atoms or the gods? In both cases it would be madness. Don't accuse anyone. Correct, if you can, the person who sins. If you cannot, put right the thing itself. If that is beyond your power, what do you gain by complaining? Nothing should ever be done without a purpose." (Marcus Aurelius, viii, 7).

"If you make a mistake, correct it with kindness, and show what the mistake is. If you cannot, blame yourself, or rather do not blame yourself." (Marcus Aurelius, x, 4).

"The wise person never quarrels with anyone, and, as far as they can, prevents others from quarrelling. On this point, as on all the others, the life of Socrates is there to serve as an example. Not only did he avoid quarrelling everywhere he went, but he also prevented others from doing so. Look at Xenophon, in the Banquet, what a number of quarrels he calmed and quelled. Look at his patience with Thrasymachus, Polus, and Callicrates. Look at this same patience with his wife, with his son, when the latter tried to refute him with his sophisms. This is because he knew all too well that no one is the master of another's soul, and that consequently, he had no will but his own. So, what is this? It is not to have the pretentiousness of forcing others to act in accordance with nature, because that does not depend on us, but to focus on, while others act on their behalf as they see appropriate, oneself living and acting in accordance with nature, by doing everything that depends on us, so that others might too live in accordance with nature… As for him wanting one's son or wife to never do anything wrong, that would be to want that what does not depend on him, does depend on him. To educate oneself is nothing other than to learn to distinguish between what depends on you and what does not depend on you." (Epictetus, *Discourses*, iv, 5).

"'But anger contains a certain pleasure, and it is sweet to return evil.' Not at all, for while it is beautiful in benefits to compensate a service with a service, it is not so to compensate an insult with an insult. There, it is shameful to be defeated. Here, it is shameful to win. Revenge is a word which has nothing human about it (and yet we confuse it with justice). The law of an eye for an eye only differs from it because it is a regulated form of revenge. Someone who returns the offence only sins with a little more of an apology.

…The most damning revenge for the aggressor is to appear not worthy of provoking revenge. Many, in asking for satisfaction for a slight injury, have only made it deeper. The great and generous human imitates the magnanimous lion, who listens unmoved to the barking of helpless dogs.

…This person gets carried away, they lose their temper. You, on the other hand, provoke them with kindness. The fight ceases as soon as one of the two leaves the scene, for it takes two to fight. If a fight breaks out, anger gets involved, the one who triumphs is the one who retreats first, whereas the victor is the loser. They have struck you, withdraw. By returning blows you provide them with the chance to give you new blows and to have an excuse to do so." (Seneca, *On Anger*, 2, xxxii).

"'It is impossible,' says Theophrastus, 'for a good person not to be angry with the wicked.' On that account, the more you are a good person, the more you are short-tempered. See if, on the contrary, you are not more gentle, more free from all hatred. Why hate those who do wrong, since it is error that leads them to it? It is not for a wise person to hate those who go astray, otherwise they would be hating themselves. Let the wise person remember how many things they have done against the law of duty, how many of their acts need leniency, and soon they will be angry with themselves. For a fair judge does not pass a different sentence in their own case than in that of a stranger. No, there is no one who can entirely absolve themselves, and every person who says they are innocent invokes the testimony of others and not their own conscience. Is it not more humane to show gentle and paternal feelings to those who sin, to bring them back, to not pursue them? If a person goes astray in the fields because they do not know their way, it is better to put them back on the right path than to chase them away. It is necessary therefore to correct the sinner by reprimand and force, by gentleness, by severity, and make them better, both for themselves as for others, not without punishment but without anger. What doctor is there, indeed, who gets angry at their patient?" (Seneca, *On*

Anger, 1, xiv).

"A good guide, when they find someone who has gone astray, puts that person on their true path, instead of leaving them there after much mockery and insults. Show therefore to this person where the truth is, and you will see how they go. If you don't show them, don't make fun of them, instead feel your own helplessness." (Epictetus, *Discourses*, ii, 12).

"They will be patient with those who are not like themselves, they will be gentle with them, kind, lenient, as with ignorant people, who go astray in the most important matters. They will not be harsh with anyone, because they will be invested with the words of Plato: 'It is always in spite of itself that a soul is deprived of the truth.'" (Epictetus, *Discourses*, ii, 22).

"Accept insults, bear the wrongs of your brother, your father, your son, your neighbour, your fellow traveller. Show us all this, so that we can see that the philosophers have really taught you something." (Epictetus, *Discourses*, iii, 21).

"If you find yourself in the middle of the crowd, tell yourself that these are games, that it is an assembly, that it is a party, and try to celebrate this party with other people. Is there indeed a sweeter sight for a friend of humanity than a large number of people? Herds of horses or oxen are a pleasure to see, it is a pleasure to have before our eyes a great number of ships, and yet the sight of a great number of people would be a pain?

But their cries stun me! – It's a trouble for your ears. But what does it do to you? Is there in the crowd a difficulty for the part of your faculties that must make use of ideas? Is there someone there who prevents you from desiring or fearing, from wanting things or rejecting them, in accordance with nature? What commotion has this power?" (Epictetus, *Discourses*, iv, 4).

"What pains you? The nastiness of people? Meditate on this principle, that reasonable beings are born for each other, that to put up with each other mutually is a part of justice, and that it is in spite of ourselves that we do evil. Finally, reflect on how it has done so many people no good to have lived with hostilities, suspicions, hatreds, and quarrels. They are dead. They are nothing but ashes." (Marcus Aurelius, iv).

"Whenever you think someone has wronged you, apply the following rule instantly: If the city is not harmed by it, I have not been harmed. If the city is offended, what is needed is not to be angry with the person that has committed the offence, but to show them what they have failed to do." (Marcus Aurelius, v, 22).

"Someone else behaves badly, what do I care? It's their business. Their ailments are their own, their actions are their own also. What I have now is what common nature wants me to have, and what I do is what my nature wants me to do." (Marcus Aurelius, v, 25).

"The best way to take revenge is to not become like the wicked." (Marcus Aurelius, vi, 6).

"We have been scratched, we have been wounded by a blow to the head, in the exercises of the palestra. We don't pretend, we don't take offence. We don't distrust the person who hurt us as a traitor. We just watch out for them, not as an enemy, not because we suspect them. We avoid them, we do not hate them. This is how it is necessary to behave in all the other encounters of life. Let's not be too careful about actions, let's pretend that we are in the palestra. It is permissible, as I have said, to avoid certain people without nevertheless feeling either suspicion or hatred." (Marcus Aurelius, vi, 20).

"It is particular to being human to love even those who offend us. We come to this point when we reflect that humans are our kin, that it is through ignorance, in spite of themselves, that they sin, that soon we will all die, and above all, that they have done no harm to us. Indeed, your soul has not been made worse than it was before." (Marcus Aurelius, vii, 22).

"You might not be angry with the stupid and ungrateful, more than that, you can do them good." (Marcus Aurelius, viii, 8).

"People are made for each other: therefore correct them or bear with them" (Marcus Aurelius, 59).

"Penetrate into the soul of each person, but allow others to also penetrate into your soul." (Marcus Aurelius, viii, 61).

"Let's leave other people's faults where they are." (Marcus Aurelius, ix, 20).

"If you can, correct others. In the contrary case that you cannot, remember that you have been given kindness in order to exercise it toward them. The gods themselves are kind toward these beings, they help them, so great is their goodness, to acquire health, wealth, and glory. You may do as the gods do, or tell me who is stopping you." (Marcus Aurelius, ix, 11).

"If others criticise you, or hate you, or clamour against you, enter into their souls, penetrate to the bottom, and see what they are. You will see that you don't have to torment yourself in order to make them take some opinion of you. Nature has made you friends. The gods themselves come to their aid in every way, through dreams, oracles, and in order to ensure that they have precisely the goods that are the object of their care." (Marcus Aurelius, 27).

"If they have sinned, the evil is in them, but perhaps they have not sinned." (Marcus Aurelius, 38).

"It is in your power, through your lessons,

to set straight anyone who has strayed from the right path, for every mistake is a deviation from the goal we set ourselves, a real aberration. What harm has therefore been done to you? What more do you ask of yourself in doing good by all people. Is it not enough for you to have done something in accordance with your nature, and do you want to be rewarded for it? It is as if the eye asked for a reward because it sees, or the feet because they walk. Just as these parts of the body have been made for a certain function, and in performing the function required by their structure they do what is proper to them, so humans, born to do good, do it when they render a service, when they come to the help of others in things that in themselves are nothing, only what their composition consists of, they have achieved their purpose." (Marcus Aurelius, ix, 42).

"Remember, when you feel anger or indignation, that human life is only an imperceptible moment, and that soon we will all be in the grave.

That it is not their actions that cause our torment, for they remain only in the mind that produced them, but that it is our opinions that torture us. Erase the opinion, then. Stop judging their actions as if they were bad for you, and your anger will have passed.

That kindness is invincible, provided that it is sincere, unconcealed, and natural. For what could the 'meanest of humans' do to you, if you persevered in treating them gently? If in the moment, you urged them peacefully, and if you were to give them without anger, when they try to do you harm, lessons like these: 'No, my child! We were born for something else! It is not I who will afflict harm, it is you who are doing it to yourself, my child!' Show them skilfully, through a general consideration, that this is the rule, that neither bees act like them, nor any of the animals that naturally live in groups. Don't mock or insult them, but give the air of genuine affection, of a heart that is not soured by anger. Do this not like a pedant, not to make yourself admired by those who are there, but keep them alone in mind, even if there were other witnesses there.

Remember these points as if they were inspirations from the Muses, and begin at last, while you live, to be a human. But it's necessary to avoid flattering them, as much as showing them anger. On one side or the other you are failing society and exposing yourself to doing evil. In fits of anger, have at hand this truth, that it is not worthy of a person to emancipate themselves, that kindness and goodness, while they are more in keeping with their nature, also have something more human, that it is there that one truly shows strength, and nerve, and not in indignation and resentment. For the closer this conduct comes to insensitivity, the more it resembles strength." (Marcus Aurelius, xi, 18).

Chapter 4

Active Charity

Kindness, Benevolence, Generosity

The principle of active charity for the Stoics is the love that should unite all humans, since nature has made them limbs of a single body. It is Marcus Aurelius who best expresses this idea, and who makes it best understood through the delicate distinction between the part and the limb. One can possibly accept the separation of one part from the whole without the whole being irreparably damaged. However, it does not seem to me that the same applies to the removal of a limb from the body, which involves the suffering, if not the destruction, of the whole body. There is also something abstract about the word "part", which does not convey, like the word "limb", both the idea of intense love and individuality. As Marcus Aurelius said: "We are all made to cooperate together in the same work... If you only say to yourself that you are a part, you do not yet love humans with all of your heart, you do not yet have, in doing good to them, the pleasure that pure and simple action gives, you do it only out of decorum, and not as if you were doing your own good." None of us, in contributing to the general utility, to the harmony of humanity, is absorbed by the whole. Each remains themselves and works for themselves by working for all, just as each limb draws its life and strength from the body to whose well-being it contributes. Everything we are and everything we have received must serve the universal end, which is the perfection of all, and similarly, the happiness of all. Here again, the Stoics link justice to charity: "All these goods are not yours," says Seneca. "They have been entrusted to you... Do you know how you can secure them? By giving them away." Isn't this firstly the

Active Charity

Christian idea of talents, then that of treasures placed in a good fund for eternal life, through the practice of charity? "Consider your own interests," adds Seneca, "and prepare yourself for certain and unassailable possession of these riches... As long as you keep hold of it, all of it is tarnished by crude names. It is called a house, a slave, money. When you have given it, it becomes a benefit." What seems to us to be a regrettable omission in this piece by Seneca, is that there is no mention of the most excellent riches that are in the reach of all humans, namely intelligence, the heart, and the will, treasures which humans must use for the good of all, and with the help of which they accomplish works worthy of their nature. But how much Seneca atones for this oversight in his beautiful and comprehensive definition of benefits! "What therefore is a benefit," he says. "An act of kindness brings joy to both the person who receives it and to the person who gives it. It is a voluntary and spontaneous act. What matters, therefore, is not what is done or what is given. What matters is the intention, because the benefit does not consist in the thing done or given, but in the very thought of the person who does it or gives it. Often I am greatly obliged to the person who gives me little, but does so with nobility, who equals in their heart the riches of kings, who offers me a small gift, but with a good heart, who forgets their poverty when they see mine, who has not only the will, but also the passion, to serve me, and who believes they receive when they give." With such strength of analysis, Seneca shows us here all the resources of the heart that loves and gives of itself without reserve! Seemingly the most insignificant benefit is worth more in the eyes of the Stoic than the most magnificent gifts, provided that it is inspired by love and offered with kindness and delicacy. It is the sentiment that makes deeds worthwhile. Seneca's words naturally remind us of those of Saint Paul: "Even if I have given all my possessions to the poor, if I don't have charity, I am nothing." This is also why Jesus considered that the offering of the poor widow was a greater gift than all the offerings of the rich.

But for fear that we confine ourselves to intention, Seneca hastens to say that "for the benefit to be complete, the intention and the thing are needed." It does not always depend on us to prove our sympathy to others in a very effective way, but a sincere feeling is always ingenious in showing itself, and it is only sincere if it strives to show itself through deeds. It is a sterile pity that does not put the will into activity. The will combined with the intention to do good is the only measure of the value of our actions. As Seneca says, "a good person cannot but want what they must," and what makes the person good is precisely their firm and constant will. Would their actions be less valuable because they cannot deny themselves from doing good? Well, far from it. Those who are the object of a good person's kindness know the value of that person's unalterable charity, always ready to relieve the miseries of others. Seneca gives a wide scope to charity. Speaking of the merciful person, he says: "They will wipe away the tears of others, but not their own. They will offer a hand to the shipwrecked, hospitality to the exiled, alms to the destitute… They will restore a son to the tears of a mother, they will break the chains of a slave… And they will do all this with a calm spirit and an unchanging face… They were born to be a support to all, to contribute to the public good, of which they offer a share to every person. Even for the wicked, whom they reprimand and correct according to the situation, their kindness is always accessible." We wonder why Seneca, who wants all acts of kindness to come from the heart, forbids the benefactor any outward sign of sensitivity, forgetting that it is emotion that doubles the benefit. The person knew the human heart better, who said: "Weep with those who weep!"

But Seneca has touching words about the duties of masters toward their servants, and his great soul rises above all prejudices when he recommends humanity and kindness to them, and recalls the devotion of "these respectful friends, these companions, subject, like us, to the power of fortune." Here again, it is God, the master of all of us, whom he presents for human imitation.

"The same relationship of union that the limbs of the body have with each other, is what reasonable beings, although separated from each other, also have with each other, because they are made to cooperate together in the same work. And this thought will touch your soul even more strongly if you often say to yourself: I am a limb of the body that is made up of reasonable beings. If you only say to yourself that you are a part, you do not yet love humans with all of your heart, you do not yet have, in doing good to them, the pleasure that pure and simple action gives, you do it only out of decorum, and not as if you were doing your own good." (Marcus Aurelius, vii, 13.)

"All these goods are not yours. They have been entrusted to you, and already they are waiting for another master, already they are the prey of an enemy, or the enemy feelings of another. Do you know how you can secure them? By giving them away. Consider your own interests, and prepare yourself for certain and unassailable possession of these riches, which you are going to make not only more honourable, but also more secure. What you admire, what makes you believe in your wealth and power, as long as you keep hold of it, all of it is tarnished by crude names. It is called a house, a slave, money. When you have given it, it becomes a benefit." (Seneca, *On Benefits*, 6, iii).

"What! You say that it is in order to

receive, that you give? Well, even better, it's so you don't lose. Let a gift be deposited in a place from which no return is required, but from which a return is possible. Let a benefit be stored away, like a treasure, deeply buried, which must not be dug up unless necessary. But what!? Does not the house of the rich person alone offer ample material for charity? Who would want, indeed, to reserve the name of liberality only for that which is addressed to citizens in toga? Virtue commands us to be useful to people, whether they are slaves or free, ingenuous, or emancipated, whether they have received their freedom in the proper way, or in a meeting of friends, what does it matter? Wherever there is a person, there is room for a benefit. The rich person can therefore, in spreading money even in the interior of their house, exercise their liberality, which is so called not because it is owed to free people, but because it comes from a free soul." (Seneca, *On The Happy Life*, xxiv).

"What, then, is a benefit? An act of kindness brings joy to both the person who receives it and to the person who gives it. It is a voluntary and spontaneous act. What matters, therefore, is not what is done or what is given. What matters is the intention, because the benefit does not consist in the thing done or given, but in the very thought of the person who does it or gives it.

The great difference between these two things is that the benefit is always good, but what is given or done is neither good nor bad.

It is intention that elevates the small things, gives lustre to the more common ones, and lowers the larger, more valued ones. The objects we pursue have a neutral nature, without character of good or evil. Everything depends on the intention that regulates them, directs them, and imposes a form on them. The benefit is therefore nothing that can be touched, so piety is not in the fat of the victims or the gold with which they are loaded, but in the uprightness and purity of the heart. A simple bowl, a cake of wheat, signals the religion of the good person, and the bad person does not escape impiety, even though they bathe the alter in streams of the blood of victims.

If the benefit consisted in the thing and not in the will to do good, the value of the thing would always determine the value of the benefit. That is wrong, for often I am greatly obliged to the person who gives me little, but does so with nobility, who equals in their heart the riches of kings, who offers me a small gift, but with a good heart, who forgets their poverty when they see mine, who has not only the will, but the passion, to serve me, and who believes they receive when they give, who gives as if they were sure to receive, who receives as if they had not given, who seizes, who pursues, the opportunity to be useful." (Seneca, *On Benefits*, 1, vi).

"There is no benefit except for what is offered to us first with intention, then with a friendly and benevolent intention.

It is the will that is the rule of duty in our eyes, see what conditions it must meet to make me indebted. It is not much to want something if it has not been useful to me. It is not much use to me if it is not wanted. Suppose someone wanted to give me a gift and did not do so. I enjoy the intention, but I do not enjoy the benefit. For the benefit to be complete, the intention and the thing are needed. Just as I do not owe anything to someone who wanted to lend me money but did not, in the same way I can be a friend, but not obligated, to someone who wanted to do me a favour and was unable to do it. I would also like to do something for them, because they wanted it for me.

The person who only sees themselves, themselves alone, and serves us only because they cannot serve themselves otherwise, is in our eyes on the same level as the person who gives their herds winter and summer fodder, who feeds their captives well so that they sell better, who fattens and slaughters select oxen. They are on the same level as the fencing master who trains their troop of gladiators with the greatest care. As Cleanthes says, it's a long way from a benefit to a speculation.

Nevertheless, I am not unjust enough to think that I owe nothing to someone who, by being useful to me, has been useful to themselves." (Seneca, *On Benefits*, 6, vii, xi, xii, xiii).

"One does not want less, because one cannot want. To the contrary, it is the greatest proof of a firm will, not to be able to change. The good person cannot not do what they do, because they would not be a good person if they did not do it. So a good person does not grant you benefit because they do what they must, for they cannot not do what they must. Moreover, there is a big difference between saying: They cannot do it because they are forced to, versus; They cannot not want to. If they are forced to do it, it is not to them that I owe the benefit, but to the one who forces them. But if they are forced to want because they have nothing better to want, it is they who are forcing themselves. So what I do not owe them when they are forced, I owe them when they force themselves. Let them cease, you say, to want! Here I beg you to reflect. What person is so mad as to not recognise as will that which is not in danger of perishing, of ever finding itself in opposition with itself, whereas, to the contrary, no one can appear to want so strongly as that which has a will that is constant to the point of being eternal. If we grant the will to someone who can immediately not will, are we destined to not recognise it in someone in whose nature it does not enter not to will?" (Seneca, *On Benefits*, 6, xxi).

"Clemency is the moderation of a soul that has power to avenge, or it is the leniency of a superior toward an inferior in the application of punishments… We say also that clemency is a tendency of the soul toward gentleness, when it comes to punishment.

They will wipe away the tears of others, but not their own. They will offer a hand to the shipwrecked, hospitality to the exiled, alms to the destitute. Not those humiliating alms that most of those who want to pass themselves off as compassionate people throw with disdain to the unfortunate whom they help, and whose contact disgusts them, but they will give as person to person, out of common heritage. They will restore a son to the tears of a mother, they will break the chains of a slave, they will remove a gladiator from the arena, they will even bury the corpse of a criminal. Moreover, they will do all this with a calm spirit and an unchanging face. They were born to be a support to all, to contribute to the public good, of which they offer a share to every person. Even for the wicked, whom they reprimand and correct according to the situation, their kindness is always accessible. But as for the unfortunate and those who suffer steadily, they will come to their aid with much more heart.

Whenever they can, they will stand between them and fortune." (Seneca, *On Clemency*, 2, iii).

"I was very pleased to learn, through those who have come on your behalf, that you live with your servants. This is worthy of a wise and learned person such as yourself. People will say: What? Yes, they are slaves, but they are human, they are servants. They are our slaves, but they are respectful friends, and they are our companions, if you consider that we are equally subject to the power of fortune. That is why I laugh to myself about those who hold that it is not honest to eat with the people who serve you. Why is it done this way, if not for pomp and circumstance, and because custom dictates that the master, when eating, is surrounded by a group of standing servants. They remain all night without eating or speaking, this causes them to speak badly about their master, because they do not dare to speak in their master's presence. But otherwise, the servants, who did not keep their mouths shut, and who were permitted to speak in the presence of their masters and to reason with them, freely exposed to all the dangers, gave their heads to save that of their master. They spoke during meals, but they did not say a word under torture.

Let them honour you more than they fear you. Since it is enough for God to be honoured and loved, this must be enough for masters too, for love cannot sympathise with fear." (Seneca, *Letters*, xlvii).

I

How To Give

Since charity is infinite, the benefits we can give must be without limits. This is also the opinion of Seneca. But in order that benefits are to contribute to happiness of both the giver and the receiver, they must not be dispensed haphazardly and without thought. The benefactor must use discernment, choosing the most opportune time and the most effective means to do good. Their gifts are all the more precious if they are spread by a hand that is discreet and delicate as well as liberal and generous. Seneca says: "Do you call benefits, the gifts about which you do not dare to admit to being the author?... How much further they descend into the depths of the heart, to never leave it, when they charm us less with the idea of the benefit than with that of the benefactor." We think, with Seneca, that self-respect should prevent us from accepting the services of a person that we cannot respect. Far from seeking them, we should carefully avoid opportunities to entice their benefits.

What increases the value of an act of generosity is the eagerness with which it is performed, for the promptness of goodwill proves the spontaneity of the feeling that inspires it. "To grant too late," says Seneca, "is to have refused for a long time. One must not give insolently... what can one expect from someone who offends by obliging? It is gratitude enough to forgive them for their kindness." To seek oneself in the good that one does, is, so to speak, to annihilate it oneself. "It is the hallmark of a great and generous spirit to not pursue the fruit of the good deeds, but only the good deed itself." In this way Seneca speaks to self-interested people who in lending their services, who in giving, think of receiving. He makes us understand that goodness is its own reward, and that it is a degradation to calculate the return. It is also to make the weight of one's benefits felt harshly to bestow them with an air of superiority that hurts those who receive them. The privilege of being able to give is so great that, in order to be forgiven for it, we must use it with affability and gentleness. Go to those who can call on it, spare them the trouble and humiliation of asking, anticipate their wishes and show ourselves to be so happy to answer them that they no longer have any fear of exposing them to us. Service rendered should leave no trace in the generous soul other than the desire to render further service to others. "When you have done good and someone else has received your benefit," says Marcus Aurelius, "why, following the example of fools, do you seek yet a third thing, wanting your charity to be seen, or for people to be grateful to you… Be like the vine that bears its fruit and then asks for nothing more, satisfied with having given its bunch, and preparing to bear other grapes in the season."

Those who let themselves be discouraged by the ungrateful are mainly thinking of themselves. As Seneca tells us, it is ourselves who increase the number of them by our selfishness, our pride, and our harshness. In urging us to persevere in doing good, he reminds us that "the gods do not allow themselves to be put off in their inexhaustible benevolence, because there are people who insult or forget them. They follow their nature and give their support to all, even to the perverse interpreters of their charity. Let's follow their example," he adds, "as far as human weakness allows." Elsewhere he reminds us that "the aim of a great and generous soul is to tolerate the ungrateful until it has made them grateful." He also shows us that it is unjust to be irritated by the common crime of ingratitude, which is more or less true of all humans, and that it is foolish, therefore, to be irritated by our own ingratitude. "Forgive in order to be absolved" is Seneca's conclusion. It is not necessary, in fact, to search carefully to find the vice of ingratitude in ourselves, in whatever form it manifests, whether toward God, our fellow humans, nature, and animals even, toward everything that gives us some advantage or pleasure and which we are too quick to erase from our memory. So we do not dare say that it is magnanimity to put up with the ungrateful, since our conscience makes us recognise that it is a simple duty of justice. But it is magnanimity to shower benefits on those who return evil for good, to respond to their animosity with gentleness and kindness, to keep silent about their wrongs and the generosity they have received. If anything can bring them back to good feelings, it is the virtue of the merciful, lenient human, who overcomes evil with good.

"I will not place obstacles in the way of generosity, of which the merit must increase in proportion to its number and its price. But I want discernment in this, because, by giving randomly and without thinking, you win the heart of no one. So here is my thought. Just as no movement of the soul, even if it comes from an upright will, is honest unless moderation has made it a virtue, I am opposed to generosity turning into unruliness. There is contentment in receiving a gift, even in holding out one's hands to it, when wisdom directs it to merit, but not when chance or blind turmoil throws it to the first person who comes. One must be able to broadcast it and take pride in it. Do you call benefits, gifts whose author you do not dare to admit? But how much more precious they are, how much further they descend into the depths of the heart, to never leave it, when they charm us less with the idea of the benefit than with that of the benefactor. As far as I am concerned, we should not seek the benefit of any human whom we do not respect. There is a no benefit in a gift that lacks its most beautiful aspect, the discernment of the giver." (Seneca, *On Benefits*, 1, xiv).

"Gratitude is obligatory only insofar as there is benevolence. You must not, therefore, give thoughtlessly, for you are only indebted to yourself for what you have received from someone about whom you feel indifferent. You must not give tardily, for, as in all acts of generosity, we place a great value on the willingness of the benefactor, whereby to give too late is to have refused too long. You must not give insolently, for, as it is in the nature of humans that insults are engraved more deeply in them than services, and that the good is quickly erased from their memory, stubborn as they are to retain the bad, what can they expect from someone who offends by obliging? It is gratitude enough to forgive them their kindness.

Moreover, our zeal to do good must not be slowed down by the multitude of ungrateful people. Because, firstly, as I have said, we increase that number of ungrateful people ourselves. Secondly, even the immortal gods do not allow themselves to be put off in their inexhaustible benevolence, because there are people who insult or forget them. They follow their nature and give their support to all, even to the perverse interpreters of their charity. Let's follow their example, as far as human weakness allows. Let us render services, not lend them at interest. We deserve to be deceived when, in giving we think of receiving. It is the hallmark of a great and generous spirit to not pursue the fruit of good deeds, but only the good deed itself, and still to search for the good person, even though one has only met bad people. Where would be the merit of obliging many people, if no one deceived. Virtue consists in giving. The good person does not weigh up the return from it, they have immediately reaped the reward in giving. Ingratitude should so little make us step back and become more cold-hearted about a good deed, that, if I was deprived of the hope of ever meeting a grateful person, I would rather not receive than not give. For the harm for the one who does not give comes before the harm from the ungrateful. I will say what I think. To ignore giving is to be more guilty. To not give is to be guilty sooner.

Whatever the fate of your first good deed, persist in doing good deeds for others. They will be better placed with ungrateful people, whom shame, opportunity, and example, will be able to one day make grateful. Do not grow weary. Continue your work, fulfil your role as a good person. Come to the aid of all, with your wealth, your credit, your reputation, your advice, and your salutary precepts." (Seneca, *On Benefits*, 1, i).

"Let common sense guide our generosities, having regard for the time, the place, and the person, for circumstances can make or break all the charm of a charitable act. I will be much better accepted if I give someone what they do not have, than what they have plenty of, and likewise if I give what they have sought for a long time without finding, than what they see everywhere." (Seneca, *On Benefits*, 1, xii).

"Benefits are all the more pleasing when they are thoughtfully considered, when they offer themselves and are delayed only by the discretion of the recipient. The first merit is to anticipate desire, the second is to follow it. It is even better to prevent the request. For, in fact, the honest person, in requesting, is embarrassed to speak and their forehead reddens, so the one who spares them this ordeal multiplies their benefits. A solicited gift is not a free gift, for, as our ancestors, so full of wisdom, thought, nothing costs more than what is bought by prayers. People would be more sparing with their vows if they had to make them in public, and even when making the most honourable supplications to the gods, we prefer to pray in the silence and secrecy of our hearts." (Seneca, *On Benefits*, 2, i).

"It is a humiliating word that weighs heavily and that you only express with your forehead lowered: Please. You must be gracious to your friend and to all people whose friendship you must win through your kindness. No matter your eagerness, they will come too late if they come after the prayer. You must therefore foresee their desires, and when they are understood, free them from the sad necessity of prayer. Remember that the benefits that are most pleasant and which live longest in people's hearts are those that come before us." (Seneca, *On Benefits*, 2, ii).

"Sometimes, silence or the slowness of words, which belie gravity and melancholy, spoil the most important services, since they promise air that is refused. How much better is it to add good words to good things, and to make the most of what you give, through testimonies of humanity and benevolence. To correct someone's hesitation to ask, you can add a friendly reproach: 'I blame you, when you needed something, for letting me ignore it for so long, for having used an intermediary. In my view, I am pleased to see my heart put to the test. From now on, whatever you desire, claim it as your right. This time, I forgive your rudeness.' Thus, you will make your heart esteem more than the service, whatever it might be, for which you came to ask." (Seneca, *On Benefits*, 2, iii).

"Charity is hasty, and we do quickly what we like to do. The person who delays and postpones from day to day their services, is not obliging from a good heart. They thus lose two essential things, time, and proof of their goodwill. To want late, is to not want at all" (Seneca, *On Benefits*, 2, v).

"How charming and precious is a gift, if the benefactor does not suffer the acknowledgements, if in giving they already forget that they have given! On the contrary, it is a folly to be greedy of the person to whom one renders the greatest services, and to confuse insult with gift. So you must not sour a benefit and mix it with bitterness. If you have some reproach to make, choose another time." (Seneca, *On Benefits*, 2, vi).

"What! Should I let it go unnoticed that it was from me that such and such a person received! Without doubt. If that is part of the kindness, then I will do many other things. I will give whatever it is I'm giving to many other people, which will make the original receiver guess who gave the first. Finally, do not let this person know that they have received, let me know that I have given. It's not much, you will say. It's not much, if you want to invest at interest. But if you want to give in the most profitable manner for the recipient, you will have enough testimony. Otherwise, it is not doing good that charms you, but appearing to do it. You say that I want the recipient to know. So, you are searching for a debtor. I absolutely want them to know, but what if it is more useful for them not to know, more honourable, more agreeable? Will you not change your mind? I therefore want them to know, that way you wouldn't be saving a person in the dark.

Such is the law of benefit between two people. One must immediately forget that they have given, the other must never forget that they have received. It's tearing the heart apart, it's overwhelming it, to keep reminding people of your services."

(Seneca, *On Benefits*, 2, x).

"You lose the benefits if you do not help. It is not enough to have given, you must maintain. If you want those you oblige to be grateful, you must not only give, you must love your generosities." (Seneca, *On Benefits*, 2, xi.).

"There is one person who, after doing something nice for someone, hurries for them to take this favour into account. Another person is not so hasty, but they look at the person they have obliged as their debtor, and always thinks of the service they have rendered. A third, finally, is unaware, if I may say so, of what they have done. They are similar to the vine, which bears its fruit, and then after asks for nothing more, satisfied with having given its bunch. Like the horse after the race, like the dog after the chase, like the bee when it has made its honey, the person who has done good does not shout it out to the world. They move on to another generous action, just as the vine prepares to bear other grapes in the season. Is it therefore necessary to be one of the number of people who don't know what they do? Yes, but you have to know what you're doing, because it is the nature, they say, of a person who must live in society with others, to feel that what they are doing is useful and good for society, and by Jupiter, to want those who live with them to feel it too. What you say is true, without doubt, but you misunderstand the meaning of my words. Consequently, you will be one of those about whom I have made mention earlier. They also, in fact, are driven by reasons to which their spirit gives its support. If you want to understand what my words mean, do not fear that this will cause you to neglect any action that is useful for the good of society." (Marcus Aurelius, v, 6).

"When you have done good and someone else has benefited, why, following the example of fools, do you seek yet a third thing, wanting your goodness to be seen, or to be acknowledged?" (Marcus Aurelius, vii, 73).

"No one tires of receiving good. Now, the good that we can do to ourselves, is to act in accordance with nature. So do not tire of doing good to yourself, by doing good to others." (Marcus Aurelius, vii, 74).

"Gifts are pleasing when they are offered with human appearances, or at least in a gentle and affable way. When a superior gives to me without rising above me, but with all the kindness they can, descending to my level, removing all pomp from their gift, seizing the proper opportunity, so that I seem obliged, rather by circumstance than by need. There is a way to prevent these important people from losing their benefits through their insolence. That is to persuade them that gifts do not appear greater because they are offered with more fuss, that they themselves cannot appear greater because of this, that pride is a false greatness, and that it makes people averse to even what is lovable.

You must choose your creditor with more care for debts of gratitude than for debts of money. For debts of money, it suffices to return what I have received, and in returning it, I am free and clear. But for debts of gratitude, it is necessary to pay more, and even after having returned it, I remain bound, for when I have paid, I must pay again.

Friendship warns us not to attach ourselves to an unworthy person. The same applies to the sacred bond of benevolence, from which friendship springs.

There are no benefits when one owes to whom one does not wish to owe. Before I give, I need my free will, then comes the benefit." (Seneca, *On Benefits*, 2, xiii).

"The purpose of your great and generous soul is to tolerate the ungrateful until you have made yourself grateful. By following

Active Charity

this conduct, you will never be deceived. For vices yield to virtues, if you do not hurry to hate them.

A maxim that singularly pleases you, and that you consider as sublime, is that it is shameful to be defeated in charity. But it is not without reason that it has been questioned whether it is a truth, and the thing is quite different than how your mind conceived it. For it is never shameful to be surpassed in the battles of virtue, provided that you do not throw away the weapons, and that, even defeated, you still strive to win. Not everyone brings the same strengths, the same means, the same happiness, to the execution of good work, and it is happiness that at least regulates the success of the most virtuous undertakings. The mere will to move toward the good is commendable, though another, more agile principle, could have preceded it. It is not like in the fights which are offered to the people as spectacles, where the palm announces the most skilful, though even there, fate often favours the weakest.

When it is a question of the duty that each on their side wishes to fulfil the most completely, if one has been able to do more, if they had sufficient resources at hand for their purpose, if fortune has supported all their efforts, if the other, with equal willingness, has nevertheless given less than they have received, or if they have given nothing at all, provided that they want to give back, and that they apply themselves to it with all the faculties of their soul, they will be no more defeated than the one who hands over their arms, because it was easier for the enemy to kill them than to make them retreat. This defeat that you regard as shameful, the good person is not exposed to, for they will never succumb, never give up. Up to the last day of their life, they will be ready to fight, and they will die at their post, conscious of having received much and of wanting to give back." (Seneca, *On Benefits*, 5, iii).

"No one can therefore be defeated in

terms of benefits, if they recognise that they owe, if they want to pay back, if, through their feelings, they balance the things they cannot repay. As long as they persist in this disposition, as long as they maintain this will, their gratitude is shown through outward signs. What does it matter who gives the most gifts? You can give a lot, but me, I can only receive. You have your fortune, I have my goodwill. You therefore have no superiority over me than that of a person armed to the teeth over a person armed lightly. No one is defeated in charity, because gratitude goes as far as goodwill." (Seneca, *On Benefits*, 5, iv).

"How do you deal with ingratitude? With calmness, gentleness, and magnanimity. Never let the insensitivity and forgetfulness of the ungrateful person hurt you so much that you no longer feel pleasure for having given. Never let an injustice tear these words from you: 'I wish I had not done anything!' Let even the failure of your beneficial deed still please you. The ungrateful person will always repent, if, even now, you do not.

Examine yourself to see if you have paid back all your benefactors, if no service has ever been lost in your hands, if the memory of all your kindnesses is with you all the time.

This vice about which you complain, perhaps if you search carefully, you will find it hidden in some fold of your heart. It is unjust to be angry at a common crime, it is foolish to be angry at your own. Forgive to be absolved. You can make the ungrateful person better through leniency, but you will certainly make them worse through severity. Do not harden the ungrateful person's head. If they have any modesty remaining, let them keep it. Often the overly loud voice of reproach has caused the mask of still timid ingratitude to fall. No one fears to be what they already seem to be, surprised modesty is lost.

As far as we can, let us plead the ungrateful person's cause within ourselves.

Perhaps they could not, perhaps they did not know how, perhaps they will repay. Some bad debts become good debts through the patience and wisdom of the creditor who has supported and insured them with extensions. We must do the same. Let us warm a languishing faith." (Seneca, *On Benefits*, 7, xxvi, xxvii).

II

How To Receive

All people are in turn benefactors and indebted. In whatever condition, the highest or the lowest, everyone receives from their fellow people, and it is a duty of justice as much as of charity to receive with a good heart and to keep the memory of the generosity. As we have already said, it depends more or less on the benefactor whether ingratitude or gratitude is aroused, but the nature of the person who receives is no stranger to the feelings produced in them by an act of generosity or kindness. Seneca also tells us, with a deep knowledge of the human heart, that "what especially makes people ungrateful, is too high an opinion of oneself, and the natural human failing of admiring only oneself and what is one's own, or greed, or envy. Every person is an indulgent judge of themselves. From that comes how people think they have earned everything and receive only what is due to them, and they never think they are appreciated for their true worth." Pride and egoism are always at the root of our vices. They make benefactors harsh and insolent, and obliged people ungrateful, discontented, and hateful, who turn against those who have done them good. So it seems to me that those who know how to give from the heart, know how to receive from the heart. "Of all the paradoxes of the Stoic sect," says Seneca, "this one is, in my opinion, the least strange and the least questionable: the person who has received with a good heart has given back. For, as we relate everything to intention, everyone has done everything they wanted to do… A person can be grateful by their will alone, they have offered heart for heart, and they have maintained equality, which is the hallmark of friendship. Then, a benefit is paid for in a different way to a debt. Do not wait for me to show you the payment, it is a matter which is dealt with between hearts." Yes, the simple, upright, generous soul, which gives with joy, receives similarly with joy. It cherishes the benefit, far from considering it a burden, and, while seeking to give back, it is happy to owe eternally. Thanks to the love that makes benefactors generous, affable, and gentle, and obliged parties happy and grateful, harmony is established between all the members of the human family, through the union of justice and charity.

"When we have judged that it is right to accept, let us do so wholeheartedly, let us confess our joy openly, and let it be so obvious to our benefactor that they find it an immediate reward. For it is a legitimate cause of joy to see a friend happy, even more legitimate to have made them happy. Let us show by affectionate outpourings that we have received with gratitude, let us proclaim it not only in the presence of the benefactor, but in the eyes of all. The person who has received with gratitude has already made their first payment.

There are some who only want to receive in secret. They avoid the witnesses and confidants of a benefit: these people have an ulterior motive. Just as the person who obliges must only divulge a benefit to the extent that it pleases the obliged, so someone who receives must summon the crowd. Do not accept what you are ashamed to owe. There are some people who thank you furtively, in a corner, in your ear. This is not modesty, it is a way of disowning. The person is ungrateful who, in order to give thanks, shuns witnesses.

There are people who, in business,

do not suffer the recording of their debts, do not want brokers, do not call witnesses to sign, and refuse to accept any written document. This is the behaviour of those who try hard to conceal from everyone the services rendered to them. They fear to admit them so as to appear to owe everything to their merit rather than to the support of others. They are especially sober about paying tribute to those to whom they owe their lives or fortunes, and, in fearing descending to the role of client, they lower themselves to that of ingrate.

Others speak ill of those who have done them the most good. It is less dangerous to offend certain people than to oblige them. They seek in hatred the proof that they owe you nothing. Nothing though should occupy us more than remembering our obligations, and we need to do this more than once, for only the person who remembers can acknowledge, and to remember is already to acknowledge.

What especially makes people

ungrateful is too high an opinion of oneself, and the natural human failing of admiring only oneself and what is one's own, or greed, or envy.

Every person is an indulgent judge of themselves. From that comes how people think they have earned everything and receive only what is due to them, and they never think they are appreciated for their true worth.

Greed does not allow anyone to be grateful. What is given never seems to be enough to a hope without measure. The more one obtains, the more one desires, and avarice sitting on heaps of wealth is only more ardent. Like a flame that rises all the higher, the more it springs from wider conflagration." (Seneca, *On Benefits*, 2, xxii, xxiii, xxiv, xxvi).

"Of all the paradoxes of the Stoic sect, this one is, in my opinion, the least strange and the least questionable: the person who has received with a good heart has given back. For, as we relate everything to intention,

Active Charity   107

everyone has done everything they wanted to do. Just as piety, good faith, justice, and finally each virtue, is perfect in itself, even if a person is not able to show it to the hand that gives, so they can be grateful by their will alone.

But what, they say, can the person who has done nothing, have given back? Firstly, this person has done something, they have offered heart for heart, and they have maintained equality, which is the hallmark of friendship. Secondly, a benefit is paid for in a different way to a debt. Do not wait for me to show you the payment, it is a matter which is dealt with between hearts.

We say that the person who has received a benefit with a good heart has paid it back. Nevertheless we always leave this person a debt, so that they may pay it again after having already done so. This is not a disavowal of the benefit, but an encouragement to be grateful.

Let us not therefore be afraid, nor let ourselves be overcome by this burden as if it was too heavy… Seize the blessing, cherish it, and rejoice not in what you receive, but in what you repay by remaining in debt." (Seneca, *On Benefits*, 2, xxxi, xxxiv).

www.ingramcontent.com/pod-product-compliance
Lightning Source LLC
Chambersburg PA
CBHW072059110526
44590CB00018B/3232